"*The Ten Percent Solution* is proof positive that effective books on writing need not be long or tedious. This is the best tool for writers that I've seen in many, many years. I've written fiction for thirty-five years, and taught fiction writing for twenty. During all those years I could have used *The Ten Percent Solution*. It would have helped me, and it would have saved my students a world of time.

"Ken Rand's twenty-five years of writing experience have produced a book that every writer needs. It is especially important for the writer who is still trying to break into publishing, but I would recommend it to the most experienced writers. It's a reminder that we should not get loose or sloppy."

— **Jack Cady**, author of *The Off Season*

"You *could* spend a gazillion bucks patronizing the Famous Writers School. Or you could pick up Ken Rand's economical text and pay scrupulous attention. *The Ten Percent Solution* is the Real Thing. The Write Stuff. Ken Rand and I share a common background, so I know right where he learned his hard lessons. This little book offers no magical shortcut; but it does distill many years' professional experience and common sense. When I suspect that one of my own stories is working, it's inevitably for one or more of the reasons Ken enumerates herein. The guy knows what he's talking about. If you're a long-time successful writer, pick this up as your refresher course. If you're an ambitious novice, consider this your bible."

— **Edward Bryant**, author of *Flirting With Death*

"Ken Rand has put together a succinct book packed with the kind of useful information it generally takes struggling writers years to learn on their own. *The 10% Solution* is concise, precise, and points out the kind of small but important trouble areas to help build a powerful narrative voice and a more firmly controlled style. Kudos to Ken Rand for putting his own advice into practice and offering to give others the benefit of his hard-earned knowledge."

      —**Tom Piccirilli**, author of *The Night Class*

"Ken Rand's short, no-nonsense approach to editing your own work, properly applied, will do more to make your writing appear professional than anything I've seen like it."

      —**James Van Pelt**, author of *Strangers and Beggars*

The 10% Solution

Self-editing for the Modern Writer

Titles by Ken Rand

Fiction
Through Wyoming Eyes
Fairy BrewHaHa at the Lucky Nickel Saloon
The Golems of Laramie County
Bad News From Orbit
Phoenix
Tales of the Lucky Nickel Saloon

Nonfiction
The 10% Solution
From Idea to Story in 90 Seconds
The Editor is IN

Forthcoming
Dadgum Martians Invade the Lucky Nickel Saloon!
Cut to the Bone: The Talebones Interviews

The 10% Solution

Ken Rand

Self-editing for the Modern Writer

FAIRWOOD PRESS
Auburn • Seattle

The 10% Solution

A Fairwood Press Book

Copyright © 1998 by Ken Rand

Fairwood Press
5203 Quincy Ave SE
Auburn, WA 98092
Email: **info@fairwoodpress.com**

Edited by Patrick and Honna Swenson
Designed & typeset by Patrick J. Swenson
Cover art copyright 2006 © Dora Wayland

ISBN: 0-9668184-0-7
First Fairwood Press Edition: October 1998

Printed in the United States of America

15   14 13 12 11 10 9 8 7 6 5

Acknowledgements

This book is dedicated to the memory of Georgia Ann Weston, to whom I promised this dedication 35 years ago. It could not have been written without the support and encouragement of Patrick and Honna Swenson, Dean Wesley Smith, Jack Cady, Ed Bryant, Ashley Grayson, my kids Molly, Michael and Missy, and Amy Hanson and Renee Stern, but most of all, Lynne—without her nothing would be worthwhile, and with her, everything is possible.

"In the spring of my senior year at Lisbon High—1966, this would've been—I got a scribbled comment that changed the way I rewrote my fiction once and forever. Jotted below the machine-generated signature of the editor was this *mot*: 'Not bad, but PUFFY. You need to revise for length. Formula: 2nd Draft = 1st Draft - 10%. Good Luck.'"

—Stephen King, *On Writing*, pg. 222

Contents

Secrets of the Craft
by
Dean Wesley Smith

I've got to say right off that I'm a collector of how-to-write books and essays. It's a nasty habit that got out of hand my first few years of wanting to be a novelist, and hasn't slacked off even after selling my 35th novel. I love the things, all the way from Lawrence Block's *Telling Lies for Fun and Profit*, to the current *Writer's Digest Fiction Writer's Yearbook*. Beside my computer is my "bible," *Writing the Blockbuster Novel* by Albert Zuckerman. Some of the better how-to-write books I reread often. Many just fill a wall of my home, dusted not-often-enough.

So, when Ken Rand asked me to look at his book, my response was "Great!" I was going to get a free copy of a professional writer's thoughts on how to improve writing skills. Us collectors love anything free, and knowing Ken, I expected to learn something in the process. A double bonus.

Now let me back up a moment and say a few things about Ken Rand. He's a long time professional author, a person whom I have talked with many times, and whom I admire. If you meet him you will like him. Almost everyone does. In the text he lists some of his jobs and writing credentials, so I don't need to here. But let me say clearly that Ken is a person who knows writing.

Why is knowing writing important? My opinion is that new writers (all writers, for that matter) should look for advice from writers who are farther down the publishing road. (More succssful, depending on your definition of success.) I would never listen to publishing advice from a novelist who can't sell a novel, while I've sold almost three dozen. Why would I? Newer writers have more sources of information, since just about any professional writer is farther along the publishing road than most new writers. Ken is a long, long ways down that road, folks. He's been a professional for many, many years. He's learned the way of things in publishing, and paid his dues. He's a person worth listening to. Trust me.

Now, for some reason, he has decided to write down some of his professional trade secrets in this book. And he's done it in an entertaining, sometimes funny, way. In my opinion, this book belongs on the shelves of every serious writer out there. I sold my first poem in 1974 and my first short story in 1975. I've been at this for a long, long time, and I learned some things from this book. I think just about any writer will.

Plus you'll get this cool book to put in your collection of "how-to-write" books. My guess is, you'll be reading this one over and over again.

Problem: your editor wants you to cut your 1,000 page novel or nonfiction book to 800 pages.

Problem: an editor wants your short story, article or essay, but you wrote 3,000 words and she wants 2,700. Problem: you get rejection slips with cryptic handwritten notes: "didn't grab me," "seemed to drag," "rambling," or words to that effect. Problem: your stuff isn't selling. Problem: you're just not writing at all.

Solution: you're holding it.

The Ten Percent Solution is an editing tool I've found useful—*indispensable*—for writing prose; fiction and nonfiction, any genre, any length, whether for publication or not (the process works for memos, queries, outlines and novel synopses, sales letters, papers and essays). It can help any writer, newbie or pro, make whatever she or he writes more accurate, more clear and crisp, more vivid, more compelling, sentence by sentence, paragraph by paragraph, chapter by chapter. Whatever you have to say, you'll say better with The Ten Percent Solution.

If you're trying to sell your prose, it can help you sell sooner, more often, for more money, and to bigger markets.

If you think you're a slow writer, it can help you write faster.

If you suffer from writer's block, it can help you become more productive, resulting in fewer false starts and more stories or articles finished.

Big claims for a small book.

I use The Ten Percent Solution daily, and I back my claims for its efficacy with more than thirty years experience as a freelance writer, staff writer and copywriter for radio, newspapers, newsletters, magazines, advertisers and news networks; as an editor for newspapers, magazines and newsletters; as a reporter for radio stations, newspapers and news networks; as a PR flack for politicians, daredevil shows and government agencies, and as an announcer and PR flack for stockcar races, daredevil shows, mudbogs, air shows and sports events. I've written more than a hundred short stories, a dozen novels, several nonfiction books, 200 humor columns, scores of interviews, and thousands of articles.

Some things The Ten Percent Solution can't do. It doesn't address concepts like character, theme, plot, structure and so on. You'll have to look elsewhere to master those concepts. I assume you have, or are trying to.

It also doesn't apply to poetry or to film, stage or radio scripts. The reason should become clear as you read on.

I took years to develop this technique, but you don't have to take as long. You don't have to be a reporter, editor, PR flack, copywriter, or ad peddler to learn how to use it.

In fact, as soon as you finish this book, you can try the process on your own writing, test its usefulness against your own needs and desires. Read the whole book through before you try to use the techniques described.

Most writers can get something from the process, some more than others. Newbies can get something because they haven't yet been brainwashed with a zillion versions of "The One True Way," so they're more open to possibilities. Old pros can get something out of this idea because they know writing school is never out. There's always something more to learn. That's one of the fun things about this business. Who knows where the next lesson will come from or how valuable it might be?

Still, I expect nobody will use it entirely. Some will use 90 percent, others maybe ten percent.

The Ten Percent Solution isn't meant to be gospel. It's not written in stone. In fact, I modify it for my own use from time to time, and I'll probably do so again. It's a tool, not a school. It's modular. You adapt the process to your own methods, style and goals, and you adjust it from project to project. Use what you want, discard the rest. Customize it.

This is a "how-to" book, a practical work manual. Theory supports practice, so the book is divided into two sections, theory and practice, to help you better understand how the two aspects relate. Theory comes first.

THEORY

History 101

The Ten Percent Solution wasn't born overnight. It evolved—it's still evolving as I learn more. Some history might help you understand how it came to be and why I swear by it.

I'll start with my radio days, 1968, when *Media Man!* was born.

Media Man! was intended to be five-minute humorous radio shows I'd write and produce myself, sell to radio stations and make a bundle. I wrote five or six scripts, got distracted and stopped.

I did my first real editing on my first radio job in Rock Springs, Wyoming; the owner used a newspaper Teletype at the radio station. Lesson one: I knew the difference between copy written for print, meant for the eye, and copy written for radio, meant for the ear, so I edited. It was good practice. The boss didn't care; he never noticed.

Later, I got a job peddling ads for a radio station in Price, Utah. I remember the first day on the job when I came back to the station with a sales order and sat with a pen and a legal pad to write my first real radio commercial. My boss said, "Don't do it that way. Get a typewriter, insert a copy sheet and type the spot there. It should take 30 seconds to write a 30-second spot." (Nobody knows why radio ads are called "spots.") He insisted I'd be so busy selling I wouldn't have time to do it my way. "The long way is the *wrong* way." He was right. I couldn't have done as well in the years I worked there if I'd not taken his advice. I went straight from order form to copy sheet in one step. I saved time — and I started learning to *write tight.*

Most radio commercials come in two varieties: 30-seconds and 60-seconds. I had a client who gave me copy he'd written himself, with a check already made out and a filled-out schedule. He timed each spot. Unfortunately, he read *silently.* I could never convince him he read faster silently than I read aloud (everybody does). His 30-second spots always ran 40 to 50 seconds. Talk about writing tight.

My boss insisted he get what he paid for, not a second more. My client insisted his copy run as written.

Solving the problem gave me my first look at what would become The Ten Percent Solution.

Here's what I did: he'd write: "Girls' sandals were priced at eighteen-dollars and 99-
cents. They've been reduced to only fifteen-
dollars and 99-cents." I'd change it to "Girls'
sandals were eighteen-99, now fifteen-99."
The client never really heard the difference.
The facts were there and they sounded the
same. That's all he cared about. He loved
my spots so much he complained when
somebody else took over his account who
didn't know how to give him what he
wanted—and satisfy our boss at the same
time.

(Notice I spelled out the numbers in the
above example. If I'd been talking about a
print ad, I would have written the numbers
as $18.99 and $15.99. The above shows the
announcer exactly how to say the numbers.
The client's way differs from mine. Radio
ads are written for the ear, print ads for the
eye.)

That was lesson number two.

I learned more as an assistant editor for
a short-lived small weekly newspaper in
Helper, Utah, and reporter for a large all-
news radio station in Salt Lake City.

The next big lesson came when I became
news director at a radio station in
Kemmerer, Wyoming. Big area to cover,

small towns and few people, but lots of news. I worked alone and mostly by phone. I couldn't have done it if I hadn't learned to write fast.

There's a news maxim: "I don't want it *good*. I want it *now*." When you watch the clock tick toward your next newscast, and there's nobody else but you to do the job, it's surprising how fast you can write.

I wrote fast, but I wrote accurately. I couldn't have survived if I hadn't been accurate. And clear. No mumblers allowed in the business.

My newscasts ran four minutes and 40 seconds, back-timed to the top of the hour and the network news feed. I had to get it all in. I had no time for contrived enthusiasm, chit-chat with the deejay, "commentary" or extraneous details and human interest stories. I did news.

If my listeners wanted more details than I provided, they could call up the source themselves, wait for the weekly newspaper to come out, or call me. I satisfied my listeners: the Wyoming Broadcasters Association named me newscaster of the year in 1988. Listeners were satisfied, I believe, because in the limited time I had, as I did with my shoe store client, I gave them all they wanted. I did it by being accurate, clear, tight, fast—and using The Ten Percent Solution.

History 201

That job didn't work out either (new owners again), and I went back to print. I got a job as the reporter for a small weekly newspaper in Delta, Utah. *Media Man!*, secluded in the back of my mind all these years as a Really Good Idea that might make me Really Rich someday, reemerged. I had the right format. Among other things, I was responsible for the editorial page. "Write a column," my boss said. "Write whatever you like."

For three years, *Media Man!* poked weekly fun at rural Utah and the world in general.

Somewhere along the line, I decided I was getting good and it was time to make it Really Big. The world needed *Media Man!* Visions of fame, fortune, guest shots on Larry King, and dates with tall bimbos danced in my head.

So I sent humor columns out to newspapers and magazines and got nothing back.

Something was wrong. It couldn't be because the columns weren't funny. Couldn't be. Maybe I didn't understand self-syndication. I needed help.

So I sent sample columns to columnist Bill Hall, who wrote for several newspapers in the region. I figured if I wrote a nice business letter, and included a SASE, he might give me some useful tips.

He telephoned me.

The main thing I remember from that talk—the real birth of The Ten Percent Solution—was his overall critique: "Your columns are too long."

I thought I knew about humor, and I did, a little, but hearing an authoritative source dissect a humor column like a freshman lit prof might dissect a classic sonnet or opera, was a revelation. I began to read books about how humor works. I found out why we do things in threes and why 'k' sounds are funnier than others and how to plot a buildup to a punchline. What is a punchline? And so on. I began to analyze why this was funny and that wasn't.

Humor is economical: "Take my wife. Please." "Brevity is the soul of wit," Shakespeare said. Comedians don't explain jokes. Have you ever noticed when stand-up comics stumble on a joke they drop it and move on?

It all related to what I'd learned as an ad peddler about saying 45 seconds worth of stuff in 30 seconds, about writing tight. I *knew* this; I'd practiced it as a radio reporter and PR flack. It related to what I was trying to do—and not doing well enough—in my columns. Too many words, plain and simple.

Hall's solution: "Cut your columns ten percent."

Bingo.

I looked at the columns and suddenly things jumped off the page. Redundancies, bloated phrases, big words, too many examples. Padding. *Fat.*

I set a goal: cut each column ten percent. If a column went 1000 words, I resolved to cut it to 900. After I finished a column, I'd make a pass on my computer, consolidate sentences, break a long-winded sentence into two briefer ones, shorten a three-syllable word to a one-syllable one, and so on. If I came up with 910 words, I made another pass to find at least ten more words to cut; the goal was to cut ten percent, not *almost* ten percent.

It worked. I sold columns to national markets. *Seattle Times, Buffalo News, Monterey Herald, Gauntlet* and three dozen other markets have printed *Media Man!*.

I got greedy and self-published three collections as chapbooks, made in my basement, cheap. When a reviewer compared me to Dave Barry and said, "Don't worry; Barry can't live forever," I quit the humor column business. I'm *older* than Barry!

By the time I stopped hitting myself over the head for laughs, I'd developed The Ten Percent Solution into a formal editing process that I used in everything else I wrote.

When a publisher friend asked me to write an article for a magazine she'd recently acquired, *Housewife Writers Forum*, I suggested The Ten Percent Solution. I wrote a query and set it aside. Then I revised the query with The Ten Percent Solution. I sent both, inviting her to compare. I sold the piece. Both the original query and the improved, tightened version appeared as sidebars with a challenge to her readers: "Do it better."

(Both queries are in the appendix with the same challenge.)

I later sold the article, sans sidebars, to *Heliocentric Network News*. That version, at 650 words, was less than *half* the earlier version.

(The *Heliocentric* version is also in the appendix. Check it out. Challenge: cut it fifty words.)

I no longer tear my hair out if an editor asks me to cut copy. An example: my Spider Robinson interview transcript (*Talebones* #10, Winter 1998) ran 8,000 words. I edited to 3,000 words. No problem.

Enough history, but we're not quite ready to get started. We need to do a refresher on chemistry first.

Chemistry

I used The Ten Percent Solution for eight years before I picked up *Writing the Natural Way*, by Dr. Gabriele Lusser Rico. I hadn't thumbed through the book for more than a few minutes before I realized:

- I *knew* this stuff.
- The Ten Percent Solution wasn't new. Though I applied it to my own writing in a formal process I'd developed myself, the basic idea had been around in different forms for years. Rico earned a Ph.D., lectured and had written books on her own take on the concept.
- The Ten Percent Solution relates to brain chemistry, to how we think and act as writers.

Reading the book was deja vu all over again. "I *know* this. Yeah, I know *that* too. I know *this*, but I never thought of it quite *that* way."

Rico's premise is summarized in the subtitle: *Using Right-Brain Techniques to Release Your Expressive Powers: Clustering - Recurrence - Revision - Image and Metaphor - Cre-*

ative Tension - The Trial Web - Language Rhythm.

I'd heard about left-brain right-brain stuff before, that one hemisphere is the creative side and the other is the bookkeeper — one intuitive, the other organized — but I never paid attention. I couldn't have told you which half of my brain, if any, created the prose I couldn't sell and which remembered to take out the garbage.

Rico straightened me out. She distinguishes between the two "distinctly different aspects of any creative act that sometimes come into conflict: the productive, generative, or 'unconscious' phase; and the highly conscious, critical phase, which edits, refines, and revises..."

The right brain is the creator, the left brain is the editor. Two brains, two functions. The trick, Rico says:

• "to reserve these functions for their appropriate phases" and

• "have them work harmoniously rather than conflict with one another."

In other words, get the two sides of your head to share and to play well together.

Rico concentrates on the right brain. She focuses on techniques ("clustering," "the trial web," etc.) to free right brain creativity, to get the unconscious juices flowing. The Ten Percent Solution focuses on the left brain, where the editor hangs out.

Rico has helped many people free their creativity. If you have problems getting into gear, maybe her book is for you. Her "clustering" concept alone is noteworthy.

Her techniques have limited value to me, though, because I have no problem finding ideas or getting started. (My book, *From Idea to Story in 90 Seconds: A Writer's Primer*, details my instant story generation concept.) I subscribe to the same idea service Harlan Ellison subscribes to, the service from Toledo. Ellison and other writers respond to the oft-asked and much-dreaded question, usually from a beginner: "Where do you get your ideas?" with the Toledo Idea Service gag. Or Schenectady. The point is ideas aren't hard to find. Translating them into Good Story is the hard part.

Seriously, getting ideas is not the problem. No one has come up with a new plot since before the birth of Christ. *The Thiry-Six Dramatic Situations*, by Georges Polti, covers the archetypal bases. Historian Will Durant said, "Nothing is new except arrangement." Voltaire said originality is nothing but judicious imitation.

Getting going after I've generated an idea isn't a problem. In part that's related to the discipline developed over the years as a desperate ad peddler and a reporter working solo and under deadline. In part it's due to an important aspect of The Ten Percent Solution I hadn't realized existed until I read Rico's book; the right-brain, left-brain stuff.

No, ideas are not the problem. Turning those ideas into compelling, readable — *salable* — prose is the problem. So why concentrate on right-brain creativity? I'm not saying ignore half your head. I'm saying what Rico is but in a different way. I'm saying focusing on The Ten Percent Solution will help free both hemispheres to do their thing — *in their own good time.*

To summarize: the two sides of the brain must learn to play well together.

One more class before we start writing.

Lit 101

• You're in bed reading a book and you say to yourself, "One more page, or just one more chapter; then I'll go to sleep." Then you look up and see it's four a.m. Where did the time go? You check to see if you can finish before it's time to go to work, or if you might have to consider calling in sick so you can finish the book *now* because it's so good. This author is somebody you'll want to read again.

• You're in bed reading and you realize you've gone two or twenty pages along and you can't remember what you've read. Worse, it's taken you hours to read those few pages. Your mind wandered and you just *looked* at the words. Not a good book. You may never finish it. You may never read that writer again.

• You read along thinking the protagonist is a little girl when you discover, eight pages later, she's an old woman. Or you discover she's an alien. Or the scene is on another planet. Or you thought you were in the Old West and you find you're on a space-ship. Sometimes it's done for effect, good or bad, but often the writer never intended it so.

Readers, sometimes consciously, sometimes not, can tell when a writer does something on purpose or accidentally.

One way to state The Ten Percent Solution's aim is to say it's a way to determine if what we say is intentional. Put another way, it'll help ensure we don't unintentionally say things we'd rather not have said.

These three scenarios, the Good Book, the Bad, and the Ugly, are related to The Ten Percent Solution. Here's why:

When I worked as news director at that Wyoming radio station, my UPI bureau chief in Cheyenne told me I needed to pay attention to my ACBs. Not ABCs, but ACBs. It stands for accuracy, clarity and brevity.

1) Accuracy. Always comes first for a reporter. If you're not accurate, it doesn't matter how clear you are. In fact if you're inaccurate, being clear is a liability.

2) Clarity. It comes second. Sometimes, in order to be accurate, reporters have to tangle with clarity problems. For example, reporters will say "America's Georgia," to

distinguish the U.S. state from the central Asian nation, even though the phrase might sound a bit cumbersome and unnecessary. How clear were the first radio news reports on Chernobyl, thalidomide, or fluorocarbons? Accuracy sometimes demands terms that may not seem clear at first glance.

3) Brevity. We never sacrifice the first two attributes for brevity. If the story takes extra time to tell accurately and clearly, so be it.

The three attributes are linked. When you get one, the others fall into place. I'll demonstrate that here.

What does this have to do with fiction? Mark Twain, a reporter before he wrote fiction (though he sometimes did both at the same time — *on purpose*), said: "The difference between the right word and the almost-right word is the difference between the lightning and the lightning bug."

(Twain said "Writing is easy. All you have to do is cross out the wrong word." He also said "eschew surplusage." When I first read that, I knew The Ten Percent Solution was a Good Thing.)

Accuracy is as important in fiction as it is in nonfiction. Remember the first scenario, the Good Book, the one you couldn't put down? Why was it different from the Bad one that put you to sleep, or the Ugly one that kept you backtracking from the mental image of one character or setting to another?

Accuracy and clarity is the difference. The Good Book, the one you couldn't put down, was dead-on accurate in describing character, setting and plot. You clearly understood what was happening and who was doing or saying what to whom.

The other two were the opposite. You often didn't know where or when you were, or what the characters looked like, or who spoke to whom. You couldn't tell what or whom you were reading about.

In the Good Book, lightning struck the reader. In the Bad and Ugly, he or she was bugged. Which writer do you want to be?

The matter of clarity is further complicated because, as Carl Jung wrote in *Man and His Symbols*: "Each word means something slightly different to each person, even among those who share the same cultural background.... And the difference of meaning is naturally greatest when people have widely different social, political, religious, or psychological experiences."

Length has nothing to do with it. The book you couldn't put down may have been longer, but it *read faster* even if the other was shorter—*because it was accurate and clear.* You may have sensed this.

There's more to learn about why and how The Ten Percent Solution works, but this'll do for now. I'll integrate more theoretical stuff into the next section as appropriate.

PRACTICE

The Writer

It's time to write.

When you sit down somewhere to write, put on your writer's hat.

I have a "Born to Mow" hat I wear when I mow the lawn, but I don't have a hat to wear while I write. I don't need the prop because I've disciplined myself over the years while writing in different styles, for different markets and purposes, and while developing The Ten Percent Solution, to go from writer to editor without changing head gear—*because I had to*. I had deadlines, some just seconds away. If you think having a hat might help, get one. Whatever works.

If I had a hat that said "writer" on it, I'd make sure I had another that said "editor" on it. If you try this, remember: *Never wear the two at the same time.*

Okay, you sit down and you have your "writer" hat on—figuratively or literally—and you write. Don't fret spelling, punctuation, grammar, details. Write as fast as you can. When you come across some datum you don't remember or a scene you haven't figured out yet, don't stop to look it up or check your notes. Write "tk" and move on. "Tk" is reporter talk. It means "to come." I've heard *Star Trek* writers use the term "tech" for the same purpose. Later, you'll key your search-find mode, bring up all the "tks" and resolve them.

Don't worry too much about length if you haven't done this many times. After you've written your first million words, you'll intuitively "pre-plan" length. I knew my *Media Man!* columns needed to run three and a half pages, 750 words. After a while, I almost always wrote the first draft at 850-950 words, and The Ten Percent Solution brought it down to the length I wanted.

At the Writer's of the Future workshop, we wrote a story in two days. I'm comfortable at a thousand words a day, so I concocted a story that ran about 2,000 words. Many writers aiming for an anthology with a 7500 word limit can write 7400 words before checking length. Novelists do it too.

It's a time-saver, an efficiency. I'm being vague because I think it's an unconscious process. You'll Get It after a while—and you won't be able to figure out how you did it—but for now, don't let it slow you down.

The point is, do all you can to avoid

slowing the creative process. Just write. *Write fast.* (Helpful hint: turn off your grammar and spellchecker while you write. Turn it back on to edit.)

Once you're done with the story, article or chapter, go back and use your spell-checker, check punctuation, grammar, agreement, voice, resolve the "tks." Ensure your descriptions are accurate, your scenes clear, your examples concrete and pertinent, transitions smooth. Do a general writerly edit.

Yes, this last phase is technically an "editing hat" thing, but you do it while wearing the "writing hat." The difference is attitude; you're not employing your left-brain editor function *yet*. This phase is broader, more general, done from the creator's viewpoint. It takes place before we apply the narrowly specific steps of The Ten Percent Solution.

When it feels finished, when you're sure you've been as creative as you can be, remove your writer's hat, stand up, walk around the room, change the coffee in your cup, then sit back down, put on your editor's hat, and apply The Ten Percent Solution to what you've just written.

You can fool yourself into being creative, into using the right brain and ignoring the internal critic, the left brain, while you create. You deliberately separate the functions; write first, edit later. If a hat prop helps you separate these mental functions better, try it. Write in one room and edit in another, or write on one machine and edit on another or write in the morning and edit in the afternoon. Or any combination. I wrote two novels on a word processor and edited them on a computer. Whatever works. If you find better ways, use them. (Let me know about your ways: I want to learn too.)

Writers are schizophrenic (metaphorically speaking, of course). On the one hand, we tell ourselves, "This is a work of genius! I've created Art!" Then we try to peddle it, like a widget, to *The New Yorker*, *Playboy* or *Paris Review*. Or we'll tell ourselves the story is great, but when we get a few rejections we toss it aside in despair.

Writers divide their brains into the art department, which creates the stuff, and the marketing department, which peddles it. The art department is subdivided into creative (right brain) and editorial (left brain). Writers are schizophrenic.

Successful writers separate their brain functions deliberately and at will. They write with passion, from the head and the heart. They write fast. They dispassionately edit what they've written as if somebody else wrote it.

It's no accident. Writers aren't born with the skills they have. They develop them over time, through practice, repetition. Many don't know how they do it, or can't articulate how they do it, or articulate it poorly. Some don't think about it at all; they just do it. Some may think the process is intuitive. It isn't. It can be learned and perfected. You can do it.

The Ten Percent Solution is a sequential process, steps taken in specific order. The deliberate, conscious separation of mental functions in step one.

It's easy to master, once you realize you don't have to worry about the editor hovering over the artist muttering, "What a lame sentence!" and "Did you write that junk?" and "Don't quit your day job." If you know you're going to use The Ten Percent Solution, you know in advance you've arbitrated between your two brains. You've agreed that while the writer writes, the editor shuts up. When the writer is done, he shuts up and lets the editor edit. When the editor takes over, using The Ten Percent Solution, the writer has agreed to not peek over *his* shoulder and whine, "Hey, leave that alone.

That's a cool sentence," and "This is the best stuff I've ever written," and "I quit."

If your left brain edits what your right brain creates—*as you're creating*—you might abandon the project unfinished. The left brain will win the argument. If you finish it, you might have little confidence it will sell. You might market it to lower paying markets, or not at all.

Writer's block is when the left brain bully-critic convinces the right brain wimp-artist to quit. It's like a traffic jam. Too many cars on the same road at the same time means nobody moves. Writer's block is mental gridlock.

The left brain isn't always wrong; it's the *timing* that's important. To repeat, the trick is to let one brain work without impedance from the other. The right brain goes first, creates. The left brain goes next, edits.

I free my right brain creativity by knowing my left brain will get its time at bat—*at the appropriate time*. Thus freed, I write faster and I finish.

Like rappelling for the first time—stepping off a cliff for the first time is scary—forcing yourself into a deliberate schizophrenic state might be daunting at first. If you have problems accepting the idea, consider Rico's proven success in doing it and teaching others to do it.

Reserve judgment for a while and read on. After you know more about the mechanical details of how to use The Ten Percent Solution on something you've written, maybe you'll have a little more confidence that you can do it, or at least suspend your skepticism long enough to give it a try.

The water is deep. But it isn't *that* cold. On to the next step.

The Editor

Editors, through stupidity or malice, reject the great stories we send them. They drive us nuts. We go from near-worshipful groveling when we submit to bitter cursing when they reject us. (They say they're rejecting the story, not us personally, but in our hearts, we know they're evil.)

Now and then, every writer must feel persecuted by evil editors. We all get rejected, and it hurts. I suspect that when we vilify editors, some of that psychological venom gets directed inward, toward our own editor, the left brain. Half of our head, the right brain writer, hates and fears the other half, the left brain editor. Result: reduced creativity, poor productivity, writer's block.

Attitude adjustment time: editors *enjoy* editing, and not because they're evil. Editors are people too and they love Good Story. Editing is as fun as writing.

For me, The Ten Percent Solution helps make editing fun. I look forward to it. Learn to embrace your inner editor.

(But I don't know about giving them the vote or letting them operate heavy machinery.)

So let's edit. And enjoy.

It's not enough to know something is wrong. You need to know *how to fix it*. You need the proper tools.

After I got off the phone with Bill Hall, I looked at my humor columns and tried to apply what I'd already begun to call The Ten Percent Solution. While things did jump at me and I did cut ten percent of the fat in those columns, I wasn't organized yet. I didn't know how to think about what I was doing. It took me years to organize the toolbox I call The Ten Percent Solution. It won't take as long for you to do it.

You've heard pundits say we write one chapter at a time, or one scene, or one paragraph, or even one sentence at a time? I don't recall anybody saying we write one word at a time, and maybe a typist might say we write one letter, one keystroke, at a time.

I say we write one *syllable* at a time.

Consider: we make rapid, unconscious choices as we write about which word best fits *here*. Why choose "conflagration" rather than "fire?" Why choose "drunk" over "intoxicated?" Why "peddler" instead of "advertising account executive?"

What's the difference between "reporter" and "journalist?"

The Ten Percent Solution process begins by looking at what you've written *one syllable at a time* to see if you've chosen the right word—in the right place—in the sentence and the paragraph where it appears. We start with the micro and work our way up to the macro, as you'll see.

Sound cumbersome? It isn't. We won't analyze *every* syllable (though we may look at every sentence and paragraph many times). We'll look at a selected few, in a systematic, organized way, syllables we know are indicators that something might be wrong *here*. Then we'll determine what, if anything, needs to be done.

Methodical, not cumbersome. Just the task for our stodgy left brain. Since the task is reduced to tiny, manageable components—syllables—to start with, it's easy to do.

We *start* with the micro. We don't stay there. Later, when the time is right, we'll expand to the macro, look at the whole manuscript, in logical, well-defined increments. Later. For now...

The Micro

The List

Copy this list and put it by your computer. You'll use it a lot:

ly	*very*	*smell*
of	*about*	*saw*
that	*ing*	*taste*
said	*And*	*touch*
was	*But*	*widows*
were	*like*	*aloud*
by	*ion*	*bed*
his	*felt*	*Lynne*
her	*hear*	

---

ly

Start with "ly." Put that syllable into your computer search-find function. Now start at the top of your story and key in the first hit.

Let's say the first sentence in which you find the syllable "ly" is: "She was running quickly out of the room."

Now you ask a three-part question about the word and the sentence in which it appears:

    1) do I keep it as is, or

    2) do I change it, or

    3) do I delete it?

We ask this to determine if the high-lighted word, and the sentence in which it is used is—

    1) accurate,

    2) clear,

    3) and brief.

If it meets all three criteria, then the answer is: "let it be." If we decide a better word expresses the writer's intent more accurately and clearly, we find that lightning word, thumping our handy thesaurus if we can't find it in our head. If we judge the word is redundant in the context of the sentence, we delete it.

In the sample sentence, I think "quickly" is redundant. How else does one run? So I'll change the sentence to read "She was running out of the room."

There'll always be a right answer to the question. Find it and move on.

Repeat the process in the next instance where "ly" appears. Do this until you're done testing for "ly," then go back to the top and move on to the next syllable in the series.

Notes:
• This process is computer-dependent. If you write on a "dumb" word processor, a typewriter or in longhand, you can still use The Ten Percent Solution, but it'll just take more time.

• Don't make the syllable in the search-find function whole-word or case sensitive. You may highlight a word like "analyze." The word isn't a modifier, as most words in this phase of the program are, so it's not a "problem indicator" but it does give you a chance to isolate and look at that word — to see if it's the right one, if it's accurate and clear, and if it's used in the sentence exactly the way you want it to be. Maybe you meant "study."

• Modifiers aren't all bad. When I use the word "pony" what do you see? An Indian pony or a circus pony? If I'd done a little thesaurus thumping, I might have come up with a more descriptive — more accurate — single word that didn't require a modifier.

•When you finish this phase, your copy will be a few lines shorter. One methodical step at a time, your copy is getting more accurate and clear—and briefer.

Now cue up the next syllable.

> **of**

Rather than "she was running out of the room," why not "...from the room?" Sounds better to me.

A writer I know (of) wants to eliminate the word "of" from the dictionary. He'd use "rather than" rather than "instead of." Rather than write "the mother of the boy," he'd write "the boy's mother." Good idea, but not always. The revised version is more brisk, I think. It depends. Would you change "the nature of the beast" to "the beast's nature?" Borderline case? Not really. Context dictates. Remember the editor looks at specific text by a specific writer, trying to help the writer express his or her intent the best way possible.

Here we encounter the concept of style. Some changes that seem obvious aren't really. Like "The United States of America," some forms are fixed by convention. Others are a matter of style, taste, context or other dictates.

When considering this, the editor makes judgment calls. He looks at the text, in part, for its intended audience. An article intended for the editorial page might be more formal. A story intended for juvenile readers will read differently than one meant for adults. Comic language may differ from serious.

But the writer may be trying to defy convention, mix and match for experiment or effect—Spider-Man in Victorian English, or an editorial article in a rural Western dialect. The editor, knowing this, will cooperate.

Each time you ask the three-part question about a syllable, style, convention, and similar dictates come to play. The editor knows this. Trust your inner editor.

But I wouldn't write "America's United States."

Notes:

•If you go through an entire run of a syllable and find you've not changed or deleted one instance of its use, here's what might be happening:

1) The particular syllable is not a problem for you. Different writers have different problems. Mine is wishy-washy words,

like "few," as in "he walked a few steps." I'd recommend you don't delete words from the list until your editor, conservative and skeptical, gets enough time to ensure it can be deleted without sacrificing quality.

2) You're not editing. Like the bored reader, you're just looking at the words, not comprehending them. Or maybe you've not separated the brain functions clearly (or accurately) and you're letting the writer interfere. Stop that.

3) Your piece is short and the syllable hasn't appeared much.

4) You're too good. Give this book to somebody who needs it and go make money.

•I'll use "he" as the pronoun for the writer and editor from now on. Reason: mine is a *he*. If you're a she writer-editor, translate.

---

that

Here's another indication that there may be problems in a sentence. Or: "Here's another indication there may be problems in a sentence." Even better: "Here's another problem indicator." Or informal (appropriate in some contexts, not in others. The editor knows the difference.): "Another problem indicator." Or, if I decide the modifier "problem" has been established well enough in the reader's mind and still want to be informal: "Another indicator." That was easy.

Notes:

•Too many people who say they want to be writers never start, too many who start never finish, and too many who finish one story or book stop there. They've heard that "writing is re-writing," so they spend (waste) time rewriting that one piece and never move on. They edit and give it to their writing group or workshop and take notes and go home and rewrite again, then repeat the process with another group or workshop—forever stuck in re-write mode.

What's wrong here? I suspect newer writers *don't know when to stop editing*, when to let it go and move on. The Ten Percent Solution has the added advantage in that it has *a definite end note*. When you reach the last step in the process, stop fiddling around and mail the manuscript. Then don't edit it anymore, unless some editor threatens to give you money to do so.

> **said**

In high school, I spent one English class listing substitutes for "said." I got bored after I passed a hundred. You've read manuscripts where the writer uses every euphemism possible, as if readers will see how often "said" is used and think the writer uncreative.

Phrases like "She pontificated," "He articulated," "They conversed" (or worse, "pontificated she," putting the attributer second, which is backwards), and similar ilk are called *said-bookisms*. Avoid them. If you use them, do so with care. "Said" is intended to be invisible. Like articles: "a," "an" and "the." Don't fear to use it.

Sometimes you can—or should—*not* use it.

For example, if Clark and Lois are in a room talking, how often must you say, "Clark said" and "Lois said?" Establish attribution early (for accuracy and clarity), but you don't have to do it each time Clark and Lois speaks. We got it.

Judicious editing determines how often you'll want to remind your reader who's speaking. We can lose track in a long string of exchanges, so remind us now and then with a "Clark said," or something like:

"Concentrate?" Luke frowned. "Okay, I'll try."

"Said" isn't used but we know who's talking.

If it's Lois and Lana in the same room, be more careful with attribution, as well as pronouns (two shes). Likewise if there are three or more people talking.

Notes:

•Dialogue is important in fiction. Ditto quotes in nonfiction. Some writers are better at it than others. With a background in radio and theater, I've studied and tried to understand dialogue. I've learned there's a lot to learn and I'm not done.

•Dialogue is too important to try to summarize here. Many good books are devoted to the subject. Read them. *Dialogue*, by Lewis Turco, Writer's Digest Books, is a good one. Study it.

•Ways to study dialogue: 1) read dialogue *without reading the associated narrative.* 2) read aloud. 3) read dialogue by authors you like. I recommend Elmore Leonard, Robert B. Parker, James Lee Burke, Ed McBain, Jack Cady, and Connie Willis. Make your own list. 4) read dialogue by authors you *don't* like. Compare the difference between those and authors you like. 5) select two authors at random and list how their dialogue differs.

•Dialogue may be the easiest place to lose readers. You know what's going on, but they don't. Lean over backward in their favor when doing attribution. Be reader friendly.

•I seldom subject dialogue to The Ten Percent Solution. I focus on the narrative. People speak differently than they write. Some characters may stutter, others speak with a twang, use sentence fragments, bad grammar and so on. The writer took care to ensure character is revealed through what characters say, and *how they say it*. I don't want to make characters sound like the narrative voice, or each other.

---

was

You knew how to ride a bicycle, drive a car, swim or kiss before you understood the physics involved. You don't need to know about momentum to stay on a bike or keep the car on the road. Your body will tell you about the need for oxygen when you swim. Or kiss.

So I had an "I knew that!" revelation when I found past tense slows text, makes it harder to read, and distances readers. I'll bet those Ugly books that put you to sleep used past tense a lot. The Good Book got to the point.

It's not a matter of accuracy: "She was running from the room" is as accurate as "She ran from the room." The second is clearer and brief. It's brief, yes, but why is it clearer?

Because it reads *faster* so readers have less time for their minds to lollygag and drift. Active voice involves readers' senses more directly, pulls a reader in until they get lost in the story. Passive voice distances their senses, pushes them away until they can't find the story.

Notes:

•Movie and TV writers understand active voice compels, passive repels. Study scripts, good or bad, and you'll find the writers try to keep your attention so you'll stay through the commercials. They don't want you to get bored and change channels, or wander off to read a book.

Study those commercials too. Advertisers can't afford waste when ads sometimes cost tens of thousands of dollars *per second* as they do in the Superbowl and World Series.

•The Ten Percent Solution is designed to make any prose you write more accurate, clear and brief. If you want to be unclear—for example, if you're trying to get a good grade, get a raise or cop a plea—you may want to deliberately put your readers to sleep.

Does this happen? Look at your insurance policy, lease agreement, divorce papers or your last book contract. It's possible to be excruciatingly accurate and completely opaque. Brief, in these cases, is impossible.

I'd hate to think The Ten Percent Solution is used to increase inaccuracy or reduce clarity, but any tool can be used as a weapon. An added benefit of understanding the process: from now on you'll recognize the difference soon enough to avoid getting ripped off before you read on.

•After you write a few dozen more stories or articles, you'll notice your writer chooses the passive voice less often, and when he does use it, he does so more wisely. The writer may want to submit a story so good the editor won't be able to edit it. He'll try, but it'll never happen. The editor appreciates going faster through the search-find process, but he still cuts no slack.

were

Ditto, but plural.
"Mistakes were made." Yeah, right.

by

A distancing, or "slowness" indicator. "He was hit by the pie" is more sluggish than "The pie hit him."

Where do you want to focus your readers' attention? If you want to focus on the pie, the first phrase, though more cumbersome, is more accurate. Are you sure? Maybe you want to say: "It was the pie that hit him" so your readers' will know it wasn't the *cake* that hit him. Accuracy.

Judgment calls, yes, but your editor is smart. He'll figure it out.

Notes:
•See how these indicator syllables seem to show up in herds, like teenagers at the mall? By now you may have looked at sev-

eral sentences two or three times. Before you're done, you'll see some a dozen times. This is a Good Thing.

It's like looking at a jewel through different facets, each peek revealing different aspects of the whole. The second peek may reveal a problem (and a solution) the first didn't.

In the first pass, we determined "She was running quickly out of the room" read better as "She was running out of the room." Later, we decided "She was running from the room" read even better. Before you finish, you may decide it should read "She ran," if you also determine the setting is already clear to the reader.

Why not skip from the first awkward sample directly to "She ran?" Okay with me. That's what I'd have done. You'll do this more often as you become acquainted with the process, and the next time it'll go more quickly. Now and then, the first pass, or the second or third, won't reveal the finest cut of the jewel-sentence, and you'll need a fourth look to Get It Right. That's why we go through each step of The Ten Percent Solution one at a time, even if it means we see the same sentence several times.

---

his

A modifier, as in "He had a smile on his lips." You might want to change to "He smiled." Or "His hair was gray" might read "He had gray hair." Or "He touched his hand to his head" to "He touched hand to head," or "Oy." These changes (depending on context) give us accuracy, clarity and brevity.

Mission accomplished. Let's move on.

---

her

Ditto. Is this getting easier?

Note:
•If your writer and editor are female, you may prefer to reverse the order to "her" and "his" in the list. Customize to suit.

---

very

"Wishy-washy" words are a problem with me, sort of. I have several that my editor checks in the search-find mode. "Very" is an obvious one, which is maybe why it shows up first. Consider: is "very good" good enough? Is "very, very good" twice as good? Then how much better is "very, very, very good?" "Okay" might be more accurate.

Notes:

•I didn't have a thesaurus in the radio newsroom. My listeners didn't listen with one handy, so I chose words I didn't have to look up. I wasn't trying to "dumb down" my stories. Still, I was as accurate and clear as possible. My choices were often less elegant, but elegance wasn't my goal. Accuracy and clarity was.

As a fiction writer, I have more time to let my editor chew on a word or phrase, to step back and consider options. I'm a converted thesaurus thumper.

•"Very" shows up in words like "every," which may also be a wishy-washy word. Highlight your own wishy-washy problem words like "many" or "several." Get accurate. How many, exactly? Of course, if your point-of-view character doesn't know, your editor won't force the knowledge on him or her.

> **about**

Ditto.

> **ing**

I napped in freshman English class when gerunds came up. I never heard the word until after I started using The Ten Percent Solution. So words that end in "ing" may be gerunds. Whatever.

They're also possible "slowness" indicators. Chase them down and subject them to the three-part question.

This is the longest, most tedious pass in the search-find phase. "Ing" shows up a lot. I find I change only five to 20 percent of instances where it's used. It feels good when I find a smoother, more elegant—more accurate and clear—phrase, one that's eluded me this far into the process. My editor grins and pats himself on the back when he finds these nuggets.

Notes:
•The Ten Percent Solution is modular; you can do it in phases. If you have ten minutes to edit, you just pass though one

syllable. This has unexpected benefits, all related:

•It saves time. You can effectively — *economically* — use an idle 10 or 15 minutes you'd otherwise spend playing Solitaire or Mind-drain.

•It increases productivity. Use longer time stretches to write, shorter to edit. If you have trouble starting, or finishing projects, this may help.

•Most people don't want to write when tired. You can edit tired. It's not energy intensive.

•This is consistent with right-brain left-brain thinking. I believe your right-brain works better when your body is fresh. Your left-brain, working on a syllable assembly line, can do a lot when you're tired. Chemistry.

•If you must stop during a pass, type "start here" and go fix the faucet. You'll be able to find your spot when you come back and pick up with no wasted time.

And

I study pompous twitology, other peoples' and my own. It's a hobby. And so it came to pass that I chose to add "And," whole-word, case-sensitive, to my list, because sentences that begin with "And" seem pompous. And I shall keep it in my inventory until the writer Gets It.

Notes:

•Unintentional pomposity is as bad as unintentional informality. The writer doesn't want to do either. And the reader can tell. And they will tell you.

But

But I don't have a problem with "But" at the start of sentences. But if I did, I'd put it in my search-find function.

---

like

Highlighting "like," a recent addition to my list, focuses on similes like a spotlight. Cliché happens. It happens to me enough to put it in my search-find mode. If you have a problem like mine—I mean, if you have the same problem—add this to your list.

ion

"Ion" often occurs as the last syllable in long words, so keying it in your search-find mode will help determine if you got the right word. "Intoxication" may be cut to "drunk," "conflagration" to "fire," "rationalization" to "excuse."

Again, context determines tone. If it's an informal piece you're doing, you'll want to eliminate long words, which tend to sound stilted and forbidding.

Formal has a place, as in some letters to the editor, professional and trade journal writing, essays, business and legal documents. Or maybe you want to evoke a Victorian style or something similar. As a fiction writer, I try to keep my narrative voice generally informal. I want to get out of the story's way, let the words grab readers, not repel them.

Notes:

•Big words are often utilized in jargon. Avoid such utilization. Don't use jargon.

•Big words and associated phrases ("extenuating circumstances," "terminate with extreme prejudice," "negative assets"), often linked with jargon and passive voice ("mistakes were made," "the suspect was rendered unconscious," "the unlikely event of a water landing") are writers' attempts to *avoid responsibility*. Even if unconsciously, readers sense this. They distrust such non-fiction writers. Ditto fiction. Are you a storyteller or a politician?

•Obfuscation in communication contributes to significantly diminished illumination.

---

felt (heard, smelled, saw, tasted, touched)

"He saw the sun go down," or "The sun went down." "He heard the man laughing," or "The man laughed." "He felt her touch," or "She touched him." Your call.

When you show the world filtered through a character's senses, you distance your reader one degree from sensing the story environment themselves. Of course, you may want to emphasize "he *saw* the sun..." focusing on his vision rather than the sun. To bludgeon the point, checking these "sense" indicators will allow you to determine if they're exactly what your writer intended.

(insert your own problem word here)

We all have different problems. Customize The Ten Percent Solution search-find mode to solve yours.

Also you'll find problems cropping up specific to a project. For example, if you're writing about a school, highlight "school" to see if you can find appropriate synonyms. My novel *Phoenix* is set in a desert, and I saw "ground" all the time.

Don't overdo it. Remember, some words are meant to be invisible, like "said." Your editor mustn't tip the wagon too far one way or the other.

This completes the "micro" phase of The Ten Percent Solution. Now we step back, expand out, and look at the whole manuscript from different angles. We'll use different senses—visual, auditory and tactile—to see if the whole manuscript answers the three-part question against our ACB standard.

The Macro

Widows (Visual)

Pay attention to the way your words look on the page. The very *shape of letters* has a lot to do with whether a reader enjoys or even comprehends the words. Printers have known this for five hundred years.

Don't believe it? Grab a book, any book. Look at the typeface. It's serif, isn't it?

(This is a serif font.)

Now try to find a book, any book, written in sans serif.

(This is a sans serif font.)

Still skeptical?

Editors insist on standard format for manuscript submission. Most specify Courier, a serif typeface. Twelve point, please. Tiny font size gets rejected.

Need more? Once again, grab a book. Look for widows. Widows are solitary words that get stranded at the end of a paragraph, page or a chapter on a single line of type—like *this.*

You'll find some at paragraph ends, but *none* at the top of a page like the one above, chapter ends, or at the end of the book. Why? They look sloppy. And important text can be overlooked. Typesetters know this, so they take out widows.

You should too, because editors feel the same way.

Still skeptical? Okay, how about *Webster's New Universal Unabridged Dictionary*: "(Widows are) generally avoided by rewriting copy to eliminate the line or fill it out."

Have you ever submitted a manuscript where the story ends on page 29 and you write "The End" at the top of page 30? Me neither. I don't want to give editors the fidgets before they've even read my story. So I'll find a way to pull "The End" back onto page 29, or extend the story an extra few lines.

By the way, "Some editors don't want to see '-30-' or 'The End' at the end of a story," editor Patrick Swenson says. "The story ends when you get to the end of the last page! It's becoming a mark of an amateur writer in some circles." And about those widows: "When I find any single *line* (not just a single word) at the top or bottom of pages, I do my best to get rid of them."

It happens only rarely. Also rare is a page with one word at the top, the end of the last paragraph from the previous page. Annoying, and as bad as "The End" on a page by itself.

More common and less annoying are paragraph widows. In ten pages, you'll find from six to a dozen or so. These are the ones we'll chase down as the next part of The Ten Percent Solution.

Why?

1) If the "The End" widow annoys an editor, similar but lesser gaffes might prompt similar conscious or unconscious displeasure with your manuscript. It's hard enough to get published these days. Why decrease your chances?

2) Widows jolt the eye. Your readers are your best friend. Don't poke them in the eye.

Now, be vew-wy quiet. We're hunting widows.

Scan your copy for paragraph widows. One word on a line is a widow we'll subject to this exercise. Two words aren't a widow. Don't worry about one- or two-line paragraphs. These are already tight. When you find a four-line paragraph and the fourth is a widow, examine the whole paragraph, find a way to shorten it, and kill the widow. Do this with each widow paragraph.

Notes:

•Now and then, you'll find a long widowed paragraph you can't shorten. Good. It means your editor has done his job well and made *every word count.*

•The widow hunt isn't as important for accuracy, clarity and brevity as the other steps in the process; instead, it's a -polishing- phase. Here, you have a chance to shine—a touch of glory added to this paragraph or that one—and, just maybe, grab an editor's attention with your quality command of prose. A subtle distinction, probably, but I believe it can often make the difference.

Aloud (Auditory)

IF YOU TAKE NOTHING ELSE AWAY FROM THIS BOOK, TAKE THIS: READ YOUR COPY ALOUD. MAKE IT A HABIT. IT CAN BE THE SINGLE BEST THING YOU EVER DO TO IMPROVE YOUR WRITING.

I seldom went on the air with news or ad copy I hadn't pre-read. Time and again,

I discovered factual errors and clarity glitches before anybody else did. I did it with newspaper copy. I still do it regularly and you should too.

After all the steps we've already taken, micro-examining every little syllable, some several times, it's amazing how many glitches still pop up when we read copy aloud. Facts in one paragraph don't agree with those in another. You find you've used one word three times in successive sentences. You notice four paragraphs in a row that start with a gerund. You see a series of sibilant "esses" showing up several times. Or you perceive you've produced a preponderance of "p's" in a particular paragraph.

Too-long sentences and too-short ones appear obvious. Your breath pattern will tell you. If you have to come up for air before you reach the period, the sentence may be too long. Or if it sounds like you're jogging as you read, you may have a series of short, choppy sentences.

Sometimes you want long or short sentences. The editor will know. Again, you don't want to *unintentionally* produce a clumsy or comic effect. If you did, your editor will *find out* by reading aloud and fix it.

While most readers read silently, the way words sound is significant to their enjoyment and comprehension. Words or phrases you can't read may cause your silent reader the same problem. Eschew foreign words, and those weird alien names in all consonants.

Don't you make the characters' voices in your head, too, as you read dialogue? In a *Star Wars* novel, for example, who does Darth Vader sound like in your head?

You do the same with narrative voice. If the narrative voice sounds appealing and natural to you, a person you might enjoy listening to, maybe somebody you know, then you tend to believe the story the "real" voice is telling. The story becomes comfortable *auditorily*. You'll get sucked into it.

To this day, whenever I read Mark Twain, I hear my father's voice as he read *The Adventures of Tom Sawyer* and later *The Adventures of Huckleberry Finn* to me and my brothers a chapter at a time at bedtime *that* long ago. Imagine a southern drawl done in a Boston burr. He got me hooked on Twain.

If your readers can't get a fix on the narrative voice — it's indistinct, or it keeps changing — they'll get pushed from the story.

Or they might find the voice disturbs or irritates (they may never be conscious of it), and they may abandon the book and hate it—and the author.

Accuracy and clarity is the problem. Reading your copy aloud is one way to help ensure it meets the ACB criteria.

Notes:

•"Pay attention to the sound of words."—Dave Wolverton. He studied poetry before he started writing novels.

•Jack Cady ended some paragraphs in *iambic pentameter*. He said he got the idea from Christopher Marlowe.

•Kevin J. Anderson dictates novels into a tape recorder while he's out walking.

•I don't think The Ten Percent Solution will work on poetry or movie, stage or radio scripts. If you think you can make it work on poetry or scripts, I'd like to hear from you.

•We've just looked at a story, article or chapter using our sight and our hearing to ask our three-part question against the ACB criteria. Now we involve *touch*.

Bed (Tactile)

So far we've examined our manuscript on a computer screen. Now, we're going to print out a hardcopy and look at it again.

When I worked for the newspaper in Delta, Utah, we had a procedure to find typos that got past our computer spell-checker, especially in legal notices with convoluted property boundary descriptions. One person read the original copy aloud, another followed along the typeset copy. You'd think with such caution, there'd be few or no typos.

Everybody involved in printing a newspaper, newsletter or magazine has watched the product roll off the presses — with a typo in the front page headline, or on the cover. Me too.

I told you I pre-read my radio news copy. I'll never forget hurrying off to some event, listening on the car radio to a newscast I'd recorded so I could leave early, and hearing myself report on an event scheduled ten *miles* from today.

A decade earlier, my boss sat me and a friend down and played a spot my friend had just recorded. "What's wrong with it?" my boss asked. We heard nothing wrong. Not so: the spot had no sponsor name and no address. We'd both missed the obvious.

Why do these things seem to leap off the page as they whiz past our eye? How could I read one thing and say another or not hear the obvious missing information?

We don't just *see* words when we read. We use other senses. We make mistakes because sometimes the senses we're using *right now* to read copy may be dulled, distracted or otherwise not functioning to capacity. The solution is to employ different senses in a systematic manner during the editing phase, to catch on the next pass errors that escaped the last pass.

When we saw the headline with the laughable boo-boo speed by on the press, we noticed the error we hadn't seen in layout and pasteup because we looked at the copy in a *different physical form*. The radio gaffe? I was thinking about my trip, mentally ten miles down the road, as I recorded. It took several wandering minds to miss the missing information in the recorded spot.

What I call the "bed" phase of The Ten Percent Solution is meant to help solve these problems.

Print looks different on paper than on a computer screen. Up to now, I've written in

Courier 12 point on screen. When I print a copy, I'll use Times; different typeface helps in this phase too. Also I'll read copy in a different room and at a different time of day — and in a different *posture*: I do it in bed at night, the copy on a clipboard, a red pen in hand. I'm amazed but never surprised how many changes I make in this phase. Haven't I gone over the stuff *enough*? Nope.

Now, I often put things back in I took out earlier. When my editor took them out earlier, he did so to create the best sentence possible. Now, in a broader view, I may find changing back is appropriate.

Sometimes I even *add* words if I feel they're needed to restore accuracy and clarity that might have gotten lost in earlier phases.

Then I update my computer file and print out a copy for the next, and final, phase of The Ten Percent Solution.

Notes:

•In this phase, I find "direction modifiers," like "he sat down," or "he stood up." Change to "he sat," or "he stood." There are too many such words to highlight in a search-find, but I'm alert for them now, and I catch them.

•Don't overdo it. One can "shut up," but can one "shut?" One "throws up," but one doesn't "throw," one "hurls." See what I mean?

The final phase is next. For this, I recommend you marry an English teacher.

Lynne

I did. Marry an English teacher, I mean. Lynne is my last reader before my manuscript gets aimed at somebody's desk, preferably somebody who may be in a good mood and inclined to pay for my efforts. The editor might be grumpy when he or she gets to my manuscript. I don't want to irritate them by showing them typos, punctuation, grammar errors and other gaffes. My wife catches them.

There aren't many English teachers to go around, and mine's taken, so you'll have to find a substitute, somebody you can trust to give your manuscript a final scan for typos, punctuation, errors of agreement, voice, attribution and so on. Your "Lynne" should be someone who knows the language better than you. Otherwise, why bother?

I haven't a clue where to find such a person, but I urge you to do it. Maybe you can shop around a local college. Maybe a critique group will do the trick.

Maybe *you* don't make mistakes. Maybe you're an English teacher. Still, remember the radio spot with the missing info, and get someone to double-check your work. We all make errors.

We're done. Give the art department—left and right brain, writer and editor—the day off and pass the manuscript on to the marketing department—and sell it.

Final Notes

•When I first used The Ten Percent Solution as a formal editing tool on my humor columns, I aimed to cut ten percent, not a word less. Since then I've sometimes had to, or wanted to, cut more or less. It varies from project to project.

When I write fiction, for instance, I seldom notice length. I let story dictate length and submit to appropriate markets. Exception: an anthology I want to get in has a 7,500 word limit. I have a 9,000 word story I want to get in. Cut or give up the market? Choices.

It's different with nonfiction. When an editor says she wants the article at 1,400 words and I have 3,000, I'll get out the ax. Some articles are written on spec (she'll buy it after you write it, if she still likes it) and some are commissioned (she's holding room for you, a specific length, and she expects you to produce). There usually isn't as much room to get creative as in fiction.

When you start using The Ten Percent Solution, you may want to aim for exactly ten percent, to see if you can do it. It's good practice. But remember, it's a title, not a fence.

• Don't take my word, or anybody else's, that The Ten Percent Solution works. Now that you've read the whole thing and know how it's supposed to work, it's time to test it for yourself—on your own work.

Here's what I suggest: get out an old story, one you're pleased with, but it's been in the marketplace a few times and has come back tail-between-legs. Maybe the story has gotten a dozen or more rejections, but you *still* think it's a Good Story. Maybe it's gotten personalized rejections with comments like "good writing, but not for me," or "seemed sluggish," or "didn't grab me," or "almost but not quite," or words to that effect.

This is the one to try The Ten Percent Solution on.

Print a copy of the story and set it aside. Then subject a separate file to The Ten Percent Solution. Do the whole thing as described. When you're done, print a copy and compare — the original and the one you did The Ten Percent Solution on — and see the difference for yourself.

If it works for you, use it. If you can see how to make it work for you *better*, change it. If it doesn't work for you, delete it.

•I use contractions a lot. Informal style, consistent with the book's intent and with my own preferred voice. I *did* use big words, but I hope they were well-chosen. I also used repetition, a standard teaching device. I hope the occasions didn't spill over to redundancies.

•I also played loose with grammar to retain an informal (and, I believe, more clear and informative) voice. I ain't got time for ambiguosity.

•I toyed with whether to use "The Ten Percent Solution" or "the 10 % solution" in the text. The symbols are shorter, but it looks cramped, harder to read, less clear. I discussed this with my editor, Patrick Swenson, and deferred to his judgment. You've read the results. (Lesson learned after the first edition had been in print for several months: *Books In Print* had no listing for *The Ten Per-*

cent Solution. They did for *The 10% Solution*. Numbers, I've learned, are a Good Thing in nonfiction titles, but beware the difference between the alphabetic and the numeric.)

•I wrote the first edition of this book in 11 days. It ran 14,700 words when my right brain writer finished. My left brain editor, using The Ten Percent Solution, cut it to 12,850 words in five days.

I then sent it to Patrick. His edit should be considered the last step in The Ten Percent Solution, and an insightful and welcome one. After all I'd done to ensure this manuscript was the best it could be, he *still* found ways to make it better. He pointed out areas where I was inaccurate, unclear and *too* brief. He noted instances where I did things I've advised you not to do. He found typos. (The first and second printings had a few. Even the fourth printing did. Typos happen.)

•The Ten Percent Solution is still evolving. It's fun to know there's more to learn. Now it's *your* turn: did you find anything missing here, something you may have wondered why I didn't include or mention? Or maybe you know a way to do it *better*. What is it? I'd like to know. I'm at **KRand27577@aol.com**. I'm looking forward to hearing from you.

APPENDIX ONE

•Here's the original query on The Ten Percent Solution I sent to *Housewife Writers Forum*:

Diane:

I've developed a technique I now use regularly that's earned me occasional praise for "crisp" writing. After completion of anything I write — fiction, nonfiction, humor, whatever — I go back and cut out ten percent of what I've written.

I call it "The Ten Percent Solution," and I highly recommend it to anyone who writes. It fits all genres, all styles. It works to produce tighter copy whatever the length, or whether or not the piece has an assigned length or is to be submitted complete on spec. I even use it on query letters, like this one. (Note the attached, marked "copy" in massive red letters.)

I think this could go as a 500 word short — simply a laundry list of what to do to cut copy down ten percent, (look for "of," "-ion," passive voice, long lists, etc.) or it could go to 1,500 words, if I use an example, such as this query letter, to illustrate how it gets done.

As ever, SASE enclosed for your response.

•Here is the same query revised using The Ten Percent Solution:

Diane:

A technique I use has earned some praise for "crisp" writing. After I finish writing—fiction, nonfiction, whatever—I go back and cut ten-percent.

"The Ten Percent Solution" fits all genres and styles. It tightens copy however long, or whether or not the piece has an assigned length or is to be submitted complete on spec. It even works on queries like this. (See the attached.)

I could do a 500 word short—how to cut copy down ten percent (look for "of," passive voice, "-ion," etc.) It could go 1,500 words or more, using an example like this query to show how it's done.

As ever, SASE enclosed for your response.

•Challenge: do it better.

APPENDIX TWO

•Here's The Ten Percent Solution as it appeared in *Heliocentric Network News*. Challenge: cut it 50 words:

Problem: An editor wants your article, but you wrote 3,000 words and she only wants 2,700 words. Solution: The Ten Percent Solution.

I found this idea when peddling my humor columns a few years ago. An editor said they were loose, rambling and about ten percent too long.

The Ten Percent Solution met that editor's needs. It works in fiction and nonfiction, even query letters and outlines, any style or length.

You can use it to make more sales—and more money.

Here's how:

First, when you write, don't be too concerned about length. Just put on your writer hat and write. Make sure your lead is engaging, your examples concrete, your transitions smooth, your body entertaining (or informative, if you're doing nonfiction) and your conclusion a clean wrap. Check grammar, spelling, voice, agreement—all that writerly stuff. Finish it. Then set it aside.

Second, toss away your writer hat, don your editor hat and cut your story by ten percent. As you edit, inflated prose will jump at you. You'll realize you can do with three rather than four examples, that you have a quote too many, that one can be paraphrased, another shortened.

Before you know it, you've cut ten percent. (Or so. The title is a convenience, not a fixed objective. Don't be arbitrary about this. If you go about this too arbitrarily, you may cut too much—or too little.) Best of all, what's left reads—and pays—better.

Some things to look for to trim the fat without cutting the meat:

1. *of.* When this word shows up, cut. For example, change "mother of the boy" to "the boy's mother."

2. *-ing.* Words that end in '-ing' may lead to cuts. For example, change "using fewer words will sharpen your style" to "use fewer words to sharpen your style." This also helps provide an active voice.

3. *-ion.* Words that end in '-ion' tend to appear formal. They often have three or more syllables. Look for shorter synonyms.

4. *three syllable words.* Again, longer words are often harder to read and more formal. If you can find a shorter word, use it. But be careful. When you change a word, you change meaning. Be a thesaurus-thumper and you'll see when cutting long words works and when it doesn't.

5. *contractions.* Change "I would" to "I'd." Again, this'll help condense, but be careful. Contractions may be too informal. Know when they work and when they don't.

6. *was and were.* These are passive voice. Active voice both strengthens and shortens prose. Again, be careful not to distort meaning for brevity's sake.

7. *commas.* Watch for commas in a sentence. They often flag points where whole phrases can be cut.

8. *lists.* Find padding, error and contradictions in lists.

9. *quotes.* Paraphrase where you can. Cut quotes to the bare bones. What remains will stand out.

10. *titles.* Change "Assistant Governor's Public Information Officer" to "Spokesman."

11. *adverbs.* Cut them—ruthlessly. Use the search and find function of your computer to find "ly." Often this will highlight a deleteable adverb. (Whenever you come across a highlighted, possibly questionable word, ask yourself three questions about the word:

    1) do I delete it without distorting meaning?
    2) does it say exactly what I wanted to say?
    3) would an alternate word do a better job of saying what I wanted to say?)

12. *said.* Attribution lets your readers know who is speaking your dialogue, but when Mary and John are speaking alone in a room, you needn't follow "How are you, John?" with "Mary said."

There are more. Make your own list. In time, you won't need it.

Always ask yourself, "If I cut, will it hurt meaning?" If so, leave it. If not, you've found a place to apply the Ten Percent Solution — and improve your chances to sell.

•Extra credit assignment: edit this article using the Ten Percent Solution. *Of course* you can do better.

REFERENCES

(Here are books that have helped me understand and perform the writing and editing process better. Some of these items may help you too.)

• Andersen, Richard. *Writing That Works. A Practical Guide for Business and Creative People.* New York: McGraw Hill Publishing Company., 1989.

• Atchity, Kenneth. *A Writer's Time: A Guide to the Creative Process, from Vision through Revision.* New York: W.W. Norton & Company, 1986.

• Block, Melvin. *Writing Broadcast News Shorter, Sharper, Stronger: a Professional Handbook.* Chicago: Bonus Books, Inc., 1987.

• Brande, Dorothea. *Becoming a Writer.* Los Angeles: Tarcher, 1934.

• Brown, Renni, & King, Dave. *Self-editing for Fiction Writers, How to Edit Yourself Into Print.* New York: HarperCollins, 1993.

• Caskey, C.O. *Frugal Me! Frugal Me!.* Columbia, South Carolina: The R.L. Bryan Company, 1985.

• Cappon, Rene J. *Associated Press Guide to News Writing*. New York: Prentice Hall, 1982.

• Flesch, Rudolf, PhD. *The Art of Plain Talk*. New York: Macmillan Publishing Company, 1951.

• Flesch, Rudolf, PhD. *The Art of Readable Writing*. New York: Collier Books, 1962.

• French, Christopher W., Eileen Alt Powell, Howard Angione, eds. *The Associated Press Stylebook and Libel Manual*. Reading, Mass.: Addison-Wesley Publishing Company, Inc., 1980.

• Jung, Carl G., ed. *Man and His Symbols*. New York: Dell Publishing Co., Inc., 1964.

• King, Stephen. *On Writing*. New York: Scribner, 2000.

• Lukeman, Noah. *The First Five Pages: A Writer's Guide to Staying Out of the Rejection Pile*. New York: A Fireside Book, 2000.

• Lutz, William. *Double-Speak*. New York: Harper & Row, Publishers, 1989.

• Madden, David. *Revising Fiction: A Handbook for Writers*. New York: Barnes & Nobel Books, 1988.

• McLuhan, Marshall, Quentin Fiore. *The Medium is the Massage*. New York: Bantam Books, Inc., 1967.

• Means, Beth and Lindy Linder. *Everything You Needed to Learn About Writing in High School But....* New York: Libraries Limited, Inc.,1989.

• Rand, Ken. *The Editor is IN*. West Jordan, UT: Media Man! Productions, 2006.

• Rand, Ken. *From Idea to Story in 90 Seconds: A Writer's Primer*. West Jordan, UT: Media Man!, 2006.

• Rico, Gabriele Lusser. *Writing the Natural Way*. New York: J.P. Putnam's Sons, 1983.

• Ross-Larson, Bruce. *Edit Yourself, A manual for everyone who works with words*. New York: W.W. Norton & Co., 1982.

• Rothwell, J. Dan. *Telling It Like It Isn't — Misuse and Malpractice/What We Can Do About It*. Englewood Cliffs: Prentice-Hall, Inc., 1982.

• Stott, Bill. *Write to the Point and Feel Better About Your Writing*. New York: Columbia University Press., 1984.

• Strunk, William Jr., and E.B. White. *The Elements of Style*. New York: MacMillan Publishing Co., Inc., 1979.

• Twain, Mark. "Cooper's Prose Style." *New Uncensored Writings by Mark Twain Letters From the Earth*, Bernard DeVoto, ed. New York: Harper & Row Publishers, Inc., 1938.

• United Press International. *UPI Stylebook, The Authoritative Handbook for Writers, Editors & News Directors*. Chicago, Ill: National Textbook Co., 1993.

• Venolia, Jan. *Rewrite Right! How to Revise Your Way to Better Writing*. Berkeley: Ten Speed Press., 1987.

• Walsh, Bill. *Lapsing Into a Comma*. Chicago, Ill: Contemporary Books, 2000.

• Walsh, Bill. *The Elephants of Style*. New York, NY: McGraw-Hill, 2004.

• Writers' guidelines from Weird Tales, 123 Crooked Lane, King of Prussia, PA 19406-2570. (Include SASE.)

• Zinsser, William. *Writing to Learn*. New York: Harper & Row., 1988.

• Zinsser, William. *On Writing Well*. New York: Harpercollins Publishers, 1976.

About the Author

Ken Rand writes full-time from his home in West Jordan, Utah. He wrote his first million words years ago and continues to write every day. He's written and sold dozens of short stories and several novels as well as scores of interviews, hundreds of articles and several nonfiction books. He's devoted hundreds of hours teaching thousands of new writers. His web page www.sfwa.org/members/Rand/ has a biography, bibliography and excerpts from some of his work. He can be reached at KRand27577@aol.com. His philosophy: "Anybody can say you can't write. Let nobody say you don't."

Breinigsville, PA USA
16 December 2010
251619BV00001B/5/A